RETURNING HOME

....

AN OLD TESTAMENT CHRISTMAS STORY

RON SHEVELAND

I-Training

Copyright © 2013 by Ron Sheveland.

All rights reserved. No part of this publication may be reproduced, distributed or transmitted in any form or by any means, including photocopying, recording, or other electronic or mechanical methods, without the prior written permission of the publisher, except in the case of brief quotations embodied in critical reviews and certain other noncommercial uses permitted by copyright law. For permission requests, write to the publisher, addressed "Attention: Permissions Coordinator," at the address below.

I-Training
33302 Golden Meadow Ct
Yucaipa, CA 92399
www.i-training.info

Book Layout ©2013 BookDesignTemplates.com

Ordering Information:
Quantity sales. Special discounts are available on quantity purchases by churches, associations, and others. For details, contact the publisher at the address above.

All scripture quotations, unless otherwise indicated, are from the New International Version of the Bible -- Copyright © 1973, 1978, 1984 by the International Bible Society. Used by permission of Zondervan Publishing House. All rights reserved.

Returning Home/ Ron Sheveland. -- 1st ed.
ISBN 978-0-9644674-0-8-0-8

Acknowledgements

My gratitude goes to the many who contributed to this book. My wife Jodi provided, as she does for each of my books, encouragement and proofreading. Amy Nemecek polished it further with her exceptional editing skills.

As is sometimes the case, my brother Jerry and I occasionally trade sermon ideas. After I preached through the book of Ruth several years ago, he took my series, added improvements, and preached it to the church that he pastored at the time. Though I can't point out specific places, I know that his ideas influenced the final version of this book—just as his life has often helped shape mine.

A final tribute goes to Paul Newell, the pastor of *Church for Family* in Beaumont, CA. When he invited me to co-teach this series at his church he also urged me to finally finish this book. He is a valued friend and ministry partner.

"I went away full, but the LORD has brought me back empty... The LORD has afflicted me; the Almighty has brought misfortune upon me."

So Naomi returned from Moab accompanied by Ruth the Moabite, her daughter-in-law, arriving in Bethlehem as the barley harvest was beginning.

Ruth 1:21-22

CONTENTS

Episode #1: **Returning to Bethlehem**   page 1

Episode #2: **Returning to Faith**   page 21

Episode #3: **Returning to Hope**   page 35

Episode #4: **Returning to Joy**   page 55

Episode #5: **Returning Home**   page 69

EPISODE ONE

RETURNING TO BETHLEHEM

RUTH 1

When we think of the little town of Bethlehem, it is natural to focus on the birth of the Lord Jesus. But the Old Testament gives another story about the town—the book of Ruth. These two accounts are so intimately tied together, it's fair to think of Ruth as the prequel to the Christmas story.

In the sweep of redemptive history, the book of Ruth paves the way for the coming Christ child and contains a number of picturesque types of the future Redeemer. The parallels between the two Bethlehem accounts are astounding.

And besides that, Ruth is a really good read. Many have described the book as one of the best stories ever told. When Benjamin Franklin was the ambassador to France, he occasionally attended the Infidels Club—a group that spent most of its time searching for and reading literary masterpieces. On one occasion Franklin read the book of Ruth to the club, but changed the names in it so that it wouldn't be recognized as a book of the Bible. When he finished, the listeners were unanimous in their praise. They said it was one of the best short stories they had ever heard and demanded that he tell them where he had run across such a remarkable work of art. The old rascal delighted in telling them it came from the Bible.

The chronicle contains suspense, love and deep emotions. It begins with famine and funerals, draws us into the tension of the crises, and then provides a satisfying, joyous conclusion.

Did I say "conclusion"? That isn't really accurate. The final chapter reveals there is more to come. And indeed there was. The real end to the Bethlehem story is contained in the gospels with a babe in a manger.

In the same way that the book of Ruth prepared the way for the coming Christmas story, it can also prepare you for the coming Christmas season. It could be that you are not emotionally or spiritually ready for Christmas this year. Your inner wounds may make it difficult for you to visualize having the vaunted "Merry" Christmas.

To whatever extent that might be the case, you will really want to enter into this captivating narrative. To fully engage in this book your will want to read the Ruth texts listed at the beginning of each chapter. Begin now with chapter 1.

* * *

IT WAS CURIOSITY that nudged the dozing town awake. From the gray ridge on which Bethlehem sat, two figures could be seen far in the distance plodding their way toward the town. As they came closer, it was determined they were women—which only heightened the puzzle. Why would two women take a journey and why would they come to Bethlehem? Finally, the pair worked their way into the village and the speculation was lowered to whispers.

Something about one of the women drew special attention. Something familiar, maybe? Finally, the puzzle was solved. With astonishment, a voice cried out, "Could this possibly be Naomi?" Someone else quickly responded in a strong, affirmative, "It is Naomi! Naomi's returned. It's Naomi." The good news raced joyously through the city. Naomi was one who had always lived up to her name, which meant "pleasant." Over ten years before, this popular person had left the city but now she was back. "It's Pleasant," the word went out. "Pleasant has returned." It wasn't long before a group of women had gathered around Naomi all shouting, laughing and joyfully echoing her name: "Pleasant! Pleasant! Pleasant is back!"

Then the celebration was brought to a halt.

With one quick, sharp retort, Naomi silenced the crowd. "Stop it!" she cried. "Don't call me Pleasant. I'm not pleasant; I'm bitter. I am bitter because God has brought great bitterness into my life. I went away from this place full but God has brought me back empty. The Lord has afflicted me. The Lord has brought misfortune upon me."

The people fidgeted in awkward, silent shock.

It can be devastating to lose the people and things that matter to you most

There are different types of losses—the loss of a job, one's health, a dream, a relationship, a loved one... They may vary in their nature and severity, but all of them can be painful. Sometimes there are losses that go deeper than we could ever imagine they could possibly go. We see other people go through them and we give them our words of consolation. But when we arrive at that point we are totally persuaded in our mind that this loss is much deeper than anyone else could ever imagine. No one understands how we feel.

The first chapter of Ruth is a narrative of loss. The Naomi who came back to Bethlehem was a woman in incredible pain, someone who felt like she'd been totally emptied of everything in life that really mattered to her. As we work our way through the chapter we unearth loss after loss after loss, and we wonder why one woman would have such pain thrust upon her.

The opening verses begin with the loss of her home. "In the days when the judges ruled..." That was a four hundred year period of ups and downs when anarchy reigned. "There was a famine in the land. The man from Bethlehem in Judah together with his wife and two sons went to live for a while in the country of Moab." Try to imagine Naomi's heart when her husband Elimelek came to her and said, "Honey, we're going to have to leave."

There is great difficulty in understanding what people go through when they move. I suppose that's because it varies for each of us. Some of us are comfortable with transitions and moving doesn't feel very traumatic. In contrast, some of you have only moved across town and yet have declared, "I'm never going to move again!"

Moves are toughest when they force people to leave a culture in which they feel comfortable and transfer to a foreign setting where they don't fit in. They lose their friends, support system, and even their sense of security.

There is a feeling of being dislodged from safe moorings and set afloat in a sea of gray waves. The people around you simply can't understand because they are at home.

Some of you have experienced this and know a little of what Naomi was going through. But take your experience and increase it tenfold. Here was a woman who was part of the "children of God"—the people of Israel. Their faith and family roots were so deep that an uprooting move to another country had to be devastating.

Naomi didn't simply move from one location to another location or from one culture to another culture. She left her people to go to Moab—a land that God had cursed. The Moabites were a people that had disobeyed God and lived with the consequences of His disfavor. Naomi understood that Elimelek had made the move for the welfare of their family but she had kept repeating to herself, "It will only be for a while... only for a while. I can make it for a while." And as the pain of the move stung deeper and deeper, she continued saying, "But it will only be for a while."

Then she experienced an even worse loss. Elimelek, the man she loved, her soul mate, the one she was dependent upon, her anchor in this heathen environment, was struck down. He was dead; she was left. I've never experienced anything so severe. The closest I've come to it was losing my parents. And although the pain of that loss continues to make my heart wince when I think of it, I still don't think that it compares to the loss of a mate in his or her prime. I'm not qualified to try to describe it. Some of you who have lost a husband or a wife are more qualified but you still struggle with putting your feelings into words, don't you?

The pain of grief is so great it's hard to articulate and even as your words stumble forth there is no way that you can express the real scars that exist on the inside. There is no describing it.

C.S. Lewis was a confirmed bachelor for years until 1956 when he married a poet from America. Four years later she suddenly died of cancer. His pain was so intense that his self-imposed therapy was wandering the empty house, grabbing empty notebooks, scribbling here and there, and keeping a haphazard journal of his feelings. This surfaced in his book, *A Grief Observed*. At first he was so ashamed of it he didn't even publish it under his own name; he used a pseudonym. This book really isn't much when it comes to theology but it does reveal the genuine feelings of a man in pain. The pages consist of a running dialogue of his hurt:

> No one ever told me that grief felt so like fear. I'm not afraid but the sensation is like being afraid. The same fluttering in the stomach, the same restlessness, the yawning. I keep on swallowing.

At other times it feels like being mildly drunk or concussed. There is a sort of invisible blanket between the world and me. I find it hard to take in what anyone says. Or perhaps, hard to want to take it in. It is so uninteresting. Yet I want the others to be about me. I dread the moments when the house is empty. If only they would talk to one another and not to me.

On the rebound, one passes into tears and pathos... I almost prefer the moments of agony. These are, at least, clean and honest. But the bath of self-pity, the wallow, the loathsome, sticky-sweet pleasure indulging it -- that disgusts me.

No one ever told me about the laziness of grief. Except my job – where the machine seems to run on much as usual – I loathe the slightest effort... even shaving. What does it matter now whether my cheek is rough or smooth? They say an unhappy man wants distractions— something to take him out of himself. Only as a dog-tired man wants an extra blanket on a cold night: he'd rather lie there shivering rather than get up and find one. It's easy to see why the lonely become untidy; finally dirty and disgusting.[1]

And on he writes, page after page of pain. It's not the type of book to pick up for light reading. But some of

Returning Home

you, due to a common history, will relate to it. You've been there.

That's where Naomi was. How did she cope? She wrapped herself around her two boys, Mahlon and Kilion, and held them close. They were now the two foundation pillars on which she could rest. They found wives, Orpah and Ruth, from among the people.

For the next ten years Naomi hoped for a grandchild, one of the great hopes of any mother, but especially a Jewish mother who sincerely hoped that the Messiah would come through her lineage. But she waited and waited and waited. And then...her sons died. We don't know how; the text doesn't tell us. Perhaps a disease snatched both? Their names literally mean "sickness" and "used up." We can only speculate. But the outcome is clear. Suddenly, Naomi's boys were taken from her.

Mahlon and Kilion, gone.

Death. Loss. Emptiness.

She'd lost her home and now she'd lost her family.

Life's losses are often accompanied and amplified by inner spiritual losses

Now Naomi is in a cold, frightening survival phase. There is no welfare system for her – no widow's pension. She's at the mercy of a predatory society. If she doesn't find a benefactor or a source of income she will starve. She heard that back in Bethlehem God had blessed the people and the famine was over. Bethlehem meant the "town of bread," and she needed some. So she slowly set out with her two daughters-in-law to make their way on the long, lonesome journey.

But as her trip began Naomi realized, "There's no sense in these daughters coming along." And now, as much as it hurt, she forced herself to turn to them and tell them to go home. "Go back, each of you, to your mother's home. May the LORD show kindness to you, as you have shown to your dead and to me. May the LORD grant that each of you will find rest in the home of another husband."

In this combination of prayer and plea, Naomi reveals a core of love and spirituality. But don't assume too much. The next paragraph shows that her inner life has been deeply shaken.

Tears and weeping—the kind that shake the body and sap the soul—overwhelmed the three women. They huddled together for emotional warmth and the daughters begged to continue with Naomi. But then she pushed them back and in her impassioned response, we discover she hadn't only lost her home, family, and livelihood, but also the inner spiritual qualities of faith, hope and joy.

A loss of faith

In her emotional entanglement with all that was going on she finally admits the deepest secret of her heart—her loss of faith. Oh, not a total loss of faith in God, but a reduction of confidence in who God is and what He wants to do in her life. In verse 13 she screams out, "It is more bitter for me than for you, because the LORD'S hand has gone out against me." Then in verse 21, while speaking to the residents of Bethlehem, she complains, "I went away full, but the LORD has brought me back empty. Why call me Naomi? The LORD has afflicted me; the Almighty has brought misfortune upon me."

Some may find her words shocking and yet, if we are honest we will admit that in the midst of loss there is usually a dark, secret question: "If God is so loving and powerful, why would He allow tragedy like this to come into my life?" We may cover it up with pious little platitudes that suppress that inner feeling, yet it's often there.

A *Christianity Today* poll asked, "Have you ever felt abandoned by God? Seventy-two percent of respondents answered yes. Of those, 44 percent said, "Yes, but I relied on God's Word. And 28 percent said, "Yes, and I was devastated."

C.S. Lewis would have fallen in that second category. He wrote,

> Meanwhile, where is God? This is one of the most disquieting symptoms. When you are happy, so happy that you have no sense of needing Him, so happy that you are tempted to feel His claims upon you as an interruption, if you remember yourself and turn to Him with gratitude and praise, you will be—or so it feels—welcomed with open arms. But go to Him when your need is desperate, when all other help is vain and what do you find?[2]

Now remember, he's describing *his* feelings. He's not trying to give theology.

> A door slammed in your face, and a sound of bolting and double bolting on the inside. After that, silence. You may as well turn away. The longer you wait, the more emphatic the silence will become. There are no lights in the windows. It might be an empty house. Was it ever inhabited? It seemed so once. And that seemingly was as strong as this. What can this mean? Why is He so present a commander in our time of prosperity and so very absent a help in our time of trouble?

Not that I am (I think) in much danger of ceasing to believe in God. The real danger is of coming to believe such dreadful things about Him. The conclusion I dread is not, "So there's no God after all," but, "So this is what God's really like". Deceive yourself no longer.[3]

A loss of hope

Besides losing faith, there was also a loss of hope. That's one of the hardest things about grief. It's not just the sense of a loss of what you have, but it's also a loss of everything that can come. It's the feeling that everything has become so dark that there is absolutely no light at the end of the tunnel. All of the future looks bleak before you. There is no feeling that you can go to bed and wake up in the morning and expect life to be sunny.

All that Naomi had treasured was gone, and with them went her future...and the future of her lineage. For Jewish women, this was tragic. They all hoped that the coming Messiah might come through them. Everything before her stretched out deep, dark, lonely and despairing. So, as a result, she takes her daughters-in-law and says to them, "Return home, my daughters. Why would you come with me? Am I going to have any more sons, who could become your husbands? Return home, my daughters; I am too old to have another husband. Even if I thought there was still hope for me--even if I had a husband tonight and then gave birth to sons—would you wait until they grew up? Would you remain unmarried for them? No, my daughters."

In his commentary on Ruth, David Jackman reveals something about this conversation that most of us would miss because of our lack of understanding of Jewish customs in that day. He says that this is "a reference to the practice of levirate marriage, which is actually to feature in a very central role later in the book. If a man died without children his brother had to marry the widow to continue the family line. The first-born son of such a marriage would then be considered the dead brother's child and heir. Naomi dismisses this as totally out of the question both because of her age and the time Ruth and Orpah would have to wait for such hypothetical sons to reach marriageable age."[4]

Naomi's despair is spilled out on her daughters-in-law: "There is absolutely no hope in life for me. And if you stick with me, life will be hopeless for you as well. I can have no more husbands and I can have no more children. There is nothing left for me and there will be nothing left for you. I love you but go home."

Along with the loss of faith and hope, there was also a loss of joy...

Returning Home

A loss of joy

There is also a loss of joy. "It is more bitter for me than for you," Naomi tells Ruth and Orpah, "because the LORD'S hand has gone out against me!" And when she arrived back in the city where the people were trying to surround her with happiness and bring back the smiles that they remembered her so well for, she said, "Don't call me Pleasant," which is what Naomi means. "Call me Mara. Call me Bitterness, because the Almighty" –not circumstances—"God, the controller, has brought bitterness into my very life. I went away full but the Lord has brought me back empty. Don't call me Pleasant. The Lord has afflicted me. The Almighty has brought all this misfortune upon me."

Naomi was a transparent woman who refused to play-act or pretend she was fine. She felt like she was empty because God had turned on her, flipped her life upside down, and dropped out everything of value. On the outside, her home and family were but memories. On the inside, she'd lost faith, hope, and joy.

And that's the way chapter 1 ends.

Don't you wish there was a happier ending? Don't you wish there was a quicker ending? The problem is that there seldom is a quick solution. Those of you who have gone through great pain know the agony of having to go on and on and on and on. You grab hold of helpful verses that provide temporary help, but the next day the despair may be back.

And after a year goes by, people think that by now you should be healed and they hint that it is time to discard self-pity. And yet a birthday comes up of a lost one and the pain is all back. The memory pops back into your head and suddenly tears are coming down your face.

But all is not lost! Remember that God is still there. Always there.

Even when God feels absent He remains present through the help He provides

Where is God? You may not realize it, Naomi, but He is there. You may have lost your home, family, hope, faith, and love, but you haven't lost your God. And in spite of your words of bitterness against Him, He understands. He understands your feelings and He sympathizes with you more than you could ever imagine.

God is there. Chapter 1 begins with a famine in the land; it ends with the words that the harvest was beginning. And God's harvest was beginning in Naomi's life. She'd gone through famine and incredible emptiness but unbeknownst to her, God had already begun a replenishing process in her life. He started simply, slowly and gently, by giving her one person who would be her *friend*—that's what the name Ruth means! And Ruth displayed her love through one significant, holy act: *clinging*.

"At this they wept again. Then Orpah kissed her mother-in-law good-bye, but Ruth clung to her. 'Look,' said Naomi, 'your sister-in-law is going back to her people and her gods. Go back with her.' But Ruth replied," with words so precious that they are often used in marriage ceremonies today, "Don't urge me to leave you or to turn back from you. Where you go I will go, and where you stay I will stay. Your people will be my people and your God my God. Where you die I will die, and there I will be buried. May the LORD deal with me, be it ever so severely, if anything but death separates you and me.' When Naomi realized that Ruth was determined to go with her, she stopped urging her."

God may work differently in your life, but there is this constant that you can count on: *God is the friend who always clings to you.* And there is nothing you can do or say to Him that will shatter the loyalty He has in His heart for you. He will always be there. When your eyes are filled with tears and all is dark you may not see Him, but He is watching you and watching out for you. God will not be absent from your life. Listen to His promise: "I will never leave you nor forsake you. (Josh 1:5; Heb. 13:5)"

In Naomi's case, the Lord reached down and supported her through Ruth. Interestingly enough, this selfless friend had just had her own loss. Fellow sufferers are often the greatest helpers. And helping is often the best way to help yourself. God gave Naomi a loyal friend because God is a loyal friend. Through Ruth, God walked by Naomi's side all the way back to Bethlehem.

The text tells us that the harvest was just beginning. This would not just be true of the grain in the fields but also of the blessings that would blossom in Naomi's heart. She had accomplished her return to birthplace, but her return to faith, hope and joy was just starting.

Perhaps you need to begin a journey toward healing and vitality but you don't feel strong enough to make the trip. That's okay. To return from the devastation of deep loss, just head in the right direction and God will walk by your side and provide the help you need.

A Side Story...

Christmas

Emily controlled her tears until she opened the box containing the Nativity set. Then they fell.

In August her father had fallen from a ladder, struck his head, and after a week in a coma, passed away. The loss had been devastating, both emotionally and financially. Emily, who was headed toward her senior year of college, was forced to drop out and get a job.

She'd returned home this morning to a snow-crusted house that no longer felt like home. It had always been bright, cheery, and full of laughter. Now the drapes were drawn and the house was as dark as the features on her mother's face. It was as though mom and home were mourning together.

Emily, the baby of the family, had always set up the Christmas tree and hung the decorations together with her dad. Today she did it alone. She would have never done it for herself but she hoped that their presence would bring some cheer to her mother and the families of her brothers who would be coming later in the week.

The tree was now up and loaded with ornaments. Long red stockings hung from the fireplace mantel. Tinsel, candles and Christmassy knickknacks were on side tables. But now, when it came time to unpack the nativity set and position it at the center of the dining room table, Emily could go no further.

The set had been hand-carved by her dad. Mary, Joseph, angels, shepherds, and, of course, the babe in the manger had all been crafted by her carpenter father. Emily picked up the Joseph figurine and softly said, "Daddy, I miss you so much. Without you, this Christmas is going to be so empty." She dropped Joseph back into the box and sunk into her father's La—Boy recliner. She squeezed her eyes shut, felt further tears roll down her face, and prayed, "God, why did you take my daddy?"

This year the Nativity set would remain in the box.

EPISODE TWO

RETURNING TO FAITH

RUTH 2

Charlie Brown tells Lucy that life is filled with ups and downs. Lucy's response? "But I don't want downs. I want ups, ups and more ups."

The current wave of Christian success formulas suggests that we can live with perpetual ups. Sounds good, doesn't it? But it's not reality. Difficult times can come to everyone.

I witnessed this as a boy. As our school bus was dropping off students, it came to a house in our neighborhood lit up by the flashing lights of police cars. It was the home of Frieda, a girl my age, and her two sisters. As they got off, some kids started to joke, "Hey, Frieda, it looks like the cops have finally caught up with you." But this was no joke. The girls would soon learn that their mother had been assaulted and brutally murdered.

This was too close to home for me. If such a tragedy could happen to such a good, Christian family like Frieda's, I realized that it could also happen to mine. Terrible tragedies can afflict any of us.

And they often do.

Death. Divorce. Natural disasters. Disease. Betrayals. Job loss. Bankruptcy. Depression. Terrorist strikes. Addiction. Failure. Car accidents. Need I go on?

We can all share painful stories that illustrate each of these scenarios—and some of those anecdotes will be from our own lives. Since we know that rain falls in everyone's life, we've learned to anticipate it, but when the flood waters come surging through, it's hard not to be sucked gasping into the swirling depths.

Poor Naomi. She had lost so much—so very much. Her home, husband, sons and livelihood had all been taken away from her. And inwardly she was a broken woman who'd lost much of her faith, hope and joy.

Trials can corrode our confidence in God

By her own admission, Naomi had become disillusioned and bitter. Did she still believe in God? Absolutely. Unfortunately, some of what she now believed about

God was negative. In her mind, He was the one who had afflicted her. The very Almighty God who could have blessed her had ransacked her and robbed her of her greatest treasures.

Her providers, her husband and sons, were all gone. And the great Provider could no longer be trusted. Naomi had a damaged faith and a bleak future.

This is the woman who had returned with her daughter-in-law, Ruth, to Bethlehem. Though it offered little help, it was still the best possible place for them to eke out a living. Though there was so much in their lives that needed rebuilding, their immediate concern was just getting by financially.

In ancient Near Eastern culture, to be widowed meant that a woman would be without provisions and providers. These two widows were destitute, alone and vulnerable. There was no one to offer food, shelter, and protection from physical harm.

Through God's provisions and protection, He demonstrates that He can be trusted

Where was God in all of this? Contrary to Naomi's faulty perspective, He was there. He was behind the scenes working gently through people, places, and circumstances. And in the second chapter of Ruth, we see the Lord's hand gently and carefully moving through others to provide care. The Father touched Naomi through the devotion of a friend and the kindness of an acquaintance. The first two verses make it clear that Ruth and Boaz will be central characters in this dramatic play directed by God.

Ruth was God's agent of love. This devoted young woman could have left her mother-in-law, Naomi, and gone back to her hometown to remarry and start all over again. But instead, she chose to stay with her mother-in-law and most likely live out the rest of her life in poverty. Chapter 2 shows Ruth's sacrificial service, her brave proactivity and her hard work.

The two women arrived in Bethlehem at the time of the barley harvest. During this season of spring the people would joyfully praise God for His goodness and blessings. Ruth used the opportunity to ask Naomi's permission to glean in the fields so they would have food to eat.

Gleaning was a common practice in Ancient Israel. It was a form of charity ordained by God to care for the poor (Lev. 19:9-10, 23:22; Deut.24:19-19). Disadvantaged people like widows, orphans and foreigners would walk behind the harvesters and pick up what was left. It would allow them to store up a little grain for present and future needs.

In a small way, I personally know what gleaning is all about. My father was an evangelist who always struggled financially. He didn't go to many big churches or have some international television program that would bring in plush donations. Instead, he'd go from small church to small church and we'd live by free will offerings. Often times there would only be enough from one offering to travel to the next church. So in my early years, times were lean, and Dad and Mom were always doing this or that to try to feed our family. And one of the things we would do was glean—only in a very different way than what we see in the book of Ruth. We lived in the farm belt of Austin, Minnesota, where, during harvest time, trucks filled with corn, peas, or beans would roll into town. Dad would drive our station wagon behind those trucks and when a bump in the road or a little wind would jar or blow produce off the trucks, he would quickly stop and my brother Jerry and I would jump out, grab our future meals, and throw them in our vehicle. I have a vivid memory of our breezeway being filled with so many peas that we had a hard time getting from our house to the garage. And there mom and dad and others took off the pods and put the peas in plastic bags. We sometimes just got by as a family, but we always got by because, even through small blessings like this, God provided.

God provided for Naomi by giving a rich harvest, the benevolent right to glean, and a devoted friend. Ruth lived up to her name, which, as we saw in the last chapter, means "friend." She was the type of person who cared so much for her mother-in-law Naomi that she gave sacrificially of herself. As she arose and walked through the early morning mist towards the fields, she pushed herself beyond her apprehensions and fear. Throughout chapter 2 you find a variety of hints showing her precarious situation. She was not only a single woman without someone to protect her, but she was a foreigner, a Moabitess, someone who was despised by the people of Israel. The Moabites were hated for their perverse, false religions and their frequent attacks upon the Israelites.

The fields were filled with rough-handed laborers and there was every possibility that she could be physically attacked or even sexually assaulted. But she went because of her love for Naomi. Aside from the danger, it was difficult work. Other than prostitution, there weren't many jobs available to a woman in Ruth's situation. She chose the hard labor of a field worker. And, as is soon revealed, her dedicated work ethic was noted by others.

Ruth looked up when she heard a loud booming voice greet the harvesters and add the blessing, "The Lord be with you!"

She could tell that this man was quite popular when those in the fields enthusiastically returned the greeting. "The Lord bless you!" they answered.

Returning Home

Please imagine the narrator of this story using his fingers to sign imaginary quote marks when he says that "as it turned out, Ruth just happened to be in a field owned by Boaz." Every aspect of this story of redemption is being orchestrated by a God who is working silently but purposely behind the scenes. God would, as Boaz requested, bring blessing to the people. He would particularly bless Ruth and Naomi...and the Lord would also use Boaz as an instrument of His grace.

Boaz was from the clan of Elimelek, Naomi's deceased husband. He is described in the New International Version as a man of standing. The Hebrew term here is a little fuzzy for us and other translations refer to him as a man of wealth or valor. All would agree that he was someone people looked up to. His stellar character is demonstrated by his graciousness toward the new young woman gleaning in his field.

He immediately noticed Ruth. I wonder why? Was she beautiful? Or did he have a shepherd's heart that noticed and cared for people? Bethlehem wasn't a huge town, and a stranger might stand out. Whatever the reason, he asked his foreman about her and discovered that she was the Moabitess who had accompanied Naomi back to Israel. In a community Bethlehem's size, Boaz would have certainly heard about her already.

The overseer also disclosed that she had come that morning and politely asked if she could glean and gather among the harvesters. Seeing that such a request wasn't necessary, it revealed a noble character. And, aside from a brief rest, she had worked diligently all day long.

Boaz approached her and addressed her as his daughter. This not only showed their age difference but also evidenced his protective nature. He gently encouraged her to spend the harvest season only in his field. He assured her that he had instructed the men to treat her well and provide her with fresh water.

Ruth was astonished by his kindness and, after bowing before him, asked why she, a foreigner, had found favor in his sight.

"Boaz replied, 'I've been told all about what you have done for your mother-in-law since the death of your husband—how you left your father and mother and your homeland and came to live with a people you did not know before. May the Lord repay you for what you have done. May you be richly rewarded by the Lord, the God of Israel, under whose wings you have come to take refuge'" (2:11-12).

This response reveals a great deal about Ruth, Boaz and God. In a very short time Ruth had already won a reputation of being devoted to Naomi and the Lord. And although her mother-in-law might be having a temporary lapse of faith, Ruth is trusting her new Lord to provide refuge. Boaz shows himself to be a deeply spiritual man who desires to be used by God to bless others. And

God is portrayed as a loving protector and provider. The metaphor of Ruth taking refuge under God's wings most likely alludes to a mother hen guarding her chicks but there might also be a reference to the wings of the cherubim in the Holy of Holies (Ps. 36: 7; 61: 4).

After this first encounter between Boaz and Ruth, the relationship began to grow. At mealtime, Boaz invited her to sit with him and eat some roasted grain and bread dipped in vinegar. "Eat up, eat up," she was surely told, and she ate until she was full and even had leftovers that she would later give to Naomi. Afterwards he instructed his men to intentionally drop extra stalks for her to pick up.

God's loving-kindness will restore your trust in God

When Ruth walked home that night, she carried a bundle of grain weighing about thirty pounds. Picture the excitement when she was able to drop the heap at Naomi's feet. This amount of food was enough to feed them for a week. Then she pulled out her doggie bag and gave Naomi her supper.

Her mother-in-law, astounded by the bounty, started questioning Ruth about how she was able to gather so much grain in one day. "Where did you glean today? Where did you work? Blessed be the man who took notice of you!" The beaten down old woman was now animated with excitement.

When Ruth told Naomi that Boaz had been her benefactor, there was an outburst of gratitude. "The Lord bless him!" Naomi said to her daughter-in-law. "He has not stopped showing his kindness to the living and the dead." She added, "That man is our close relative; he is one of our guardian-redeemers."

Does this sound like the same bitter, faith-faltering curmudgeon we saw earlier? No, something is happening in Naomi's spirit. God is gently using a friend, a relative, and a harvest to care for her physical and emotional needs. We are starting to see a return to faith.

Give special attention to verse 20 where Naomi says, "The Lord bless him!" The *him*, of course, is speaking about Boaz. Then she immediately adds, "He has not stopped showing his kindness to the living and the dead." Now who is the *He* in this sentence? Frankly, neither the Hebrew nor the English renderings make it easy to be dogmatic but I tend to believe it is talking about the Lord. While we are at first inclined to take the *He* as referring to Boaz, most Bible scholars believe that the whole drift of the passage shows that Naomi is thinking of God. If that is the case, it underscores Naomi's recognition of God's grace.

God has not forsaken her or her family! His kindness is still flowing.

Returning Home

Now put your focus on the word *kindness*. The Hebrew word for kindness here is *hessed* (pronounced with a hard, almost K sounding H). It is a very special word with deep historic ramifications that the Israelites understood. It meant the loyal, steadfast, protective love that is inherent in a covenant relationship. It's the type of love that will never let go.

So here is Naomi, the woman who'd begun to believe that God had forsaken her, afflicted her, and emptied her of all blessings. But now she's undergoing a reversal of her thinking. Her eyes are opening to the fact that behind the clouds God is present, His "loving-kindness" is at work, and the covenant relationship they shared is still secure.

God had always been there and God would always be there.

With all the losses Naomi had endured, perhaps the deepest was the terrifying feeling that God had turned against her. Now through the kindness of Ruth and Boaz, she once again saw the covenantal loving-kindness of the Almighty.

This revelation was beautiful for her, and it speaks to us, as well. As dark as life gets and as deep as it seems, there is always a God who is working through people or circumstances to take care of you. His *hessed* love will never fail.

Once you grasp that, your faith will blossom. The Heidelberg Catechism puts it this way: "I trust Him so much that I do not doubt He will provide whatever I need for body and soul and He will turn to my good whatever adversity He sends me in this sad world. He is able to do this because He is almighty God; He desires to do this because He is a faithful Father."

Here is the key concept of this section: *God helps you return to faith as you open your eyes to His faithfulness.*

This book has an interesting cast of characters, but the main one is definitely Naomi. This is a story that describes her spiritual comeback. And now it has begun. She still has a long way to go; recoveries usually aren't quick. But she's on her way. She's begun to have a return to faith. Might there also be a return to hope on the horizon? Such a possibility is hinted at in the end of the chapter when Naomi declares that Boaz was one of their "guardian-redeemers." The Hebrew word translated "guardian-redeemer" or "kinsman-redeemer" is a legal term for one who has the obligation to redeem a relative who is in a serious difficulty (see Lev. 25:25-55).

Might Boaz, in that role, provide hope for their future? That is the theme of chapter 3.

The Side Story...

The Next Christmas

Emily only missed one semester of school. A grant and her savings from work had enabled her to return to college in January. Her credit card was maxed out and things were tight, but she was catching up.

This Christmas, Emily returned home with a diploma, a job offer and a picture of a boyfriend in her purse. Life was better. Not great, but better.

Her father's absence was still a shadow that seemed to absorb the twinkle of the Christmas lights. His larger-than-life personality overlapped his death and made his presence still felt. But Emily knew that she was slowly healing. She was also pleased to see that her mother, Nancy, had started going back to church and getting involved.

This year Emily set up the Nativity set and used the time to thank her heavenly Father for providing for her.

RON SHEVELAND

Returning Home

EPISODE THREE

RETURNING TO HOPE

RUTH 3

Matchmaker, matchmaker, make me a match...

It was a cold freezing day, and Arnold Fine was carefully shuffling down the slick sidewalk when he saw a wallet in the street. A quick inspection revealed no identification, just three dollars and an old crumpled letter that, according to the date, had been written sixty years before.

It was a "Dear John" letter.

The writer, Hannah, sadly told Michael, the recipient, that her mother forbade her to see him again. Nevertheless, she pledged that she would love him forever.

Apart from the address on the outside of the envelope, Arnold Fine had no clue how to find the owner of the wallet. But Arnold was on a mission. He contacted the present residents of the address who revealed that they did remember a Hannah. After a day of persistently interviewing a chain of people, Arnold discovered that she was now living in a local nursing home.

At ten in the evening, Arnold found her watching television in the day room. Hannah was a sweet, silver-haired woman with friendly eyes and a warm smile. After a brief introduction, he showed her the letter.

With a deep breath, Hannah revealed that the letter was the last contact she had ever had with Michael. Then, with upward eyes that appeared to be gazing back in time, she said, "I loved him very much. But I was only sixteen and my mother felt I was too young. He was so handsome. You know, like Sean Connery, the actor." They both laughed. Then she continued, "Michael Goldstein was his name. If you find him, tell him I still think of him often. I never did marry." She paused, then added, "I guess that no one ever matched up to Michael."

After saying his goodbye, Arnold descended on the elevator to the first floor. As he was leaving he struck up a conversation with the guard and briefly shared the story. When he pulled out the old, brown leather billfold, the guard said, "Hey, that's Mr. Goldstein's wallet. I'd know it anywhere. He's always losing it. He's one of the old-timers on the eighth floor."

Accompanied by the nursing home director, Arnold again got on the elevator, hoping that Mr. Goldstein was still awake. They found him with his lights on reading a book. After a touching conversation about the letter in the billfold, Arnold revealed that Hannah was not only alive but living in the same building. "Would you like to go see her?" With the old man's consent, they proceeded to the third floor where Hannah was still watching TV.

"Hannah," the man said with a tremor in his voice, "it's Michael. Michael Goldstein. Do you remember?"

"Michael? Michael? It's you!"

Three weeks later, Arnold got a phone call from the nursing home director who asked, "Can you break away on Sunday to attend a wedding?"[5]

Matchmaker, matchmaker, make me a match...

In this episode of the story of Ruth, we discover another matchmaker: Naomi.

We see a different side of her in this chapter. Maybe it is a more accurate picture. Perhaps it is the Naomi of old—before the tornado of pain swept through her life and whisked away her loved ones, her securities and her hopes. Now in her slow return to vitality, she is displaying some optimistic grit and gumption. Her eyes are no longer filled with tears, they are bright and twinkling. And her script has changed from woes and laments to dreaming and scheming. She emerges from her exile of gloom to cleverly plan an escapade of the heart.

I like this lady!

When all seems hopeless, God surprises us with unexpected possibilities

Naomi is now seeing an exciting possibility in an area she once thought was hopeless. While in Moab, she'd tried to persuade her daughters-in-law to stay there rather than continue with her on a dead-end street. Naomi had said, "Return home, my daughters. Why would you come with me? Am I going to have any more sons, who could become your husbands? Return home, my daughters; I am too old to have another husband. Even if I thought there was still hope for me—even if I had a husband tonight and then gave birth to sons— would you wait until they grew up? Would you remain unmarried for them? No, my daughters. It is more bitter for me than for you, because the Lord's hand has turned against me!"

Enveloped in her words are some customs with which most of us are unfamiliar. What is this talk about having further sons they could marry? Deuteronomy 25:5-6 states, "If brothers are living together and one of them dies without a son, his widow must not marry outside the family. Her husband's brother shall take her and marry her and fulfill the duty of a brother-in-law to her. The first son she bears shall carry on the name of the dead brother so that his name will not be blotted out from Israel."

The following verses are also very important for what will soon happen in this love story but let's study them later. For now, let's grasp why Naomi thought her plight was so dire.

The loss of descendants was devastating for the Jews. In some sense they believed that they lived on through their seed. It was imperative that their name go forward; the loss of descendants was a loss of continuity. There were few things in life more painful and shameful. All this was amplified by their belief in God's big promise that through the lineage of some of them would come the future Messiah.

So what happens if a man died before children were born to his wife? Is all hope gone? No, according to Deuteronomy 25, another brother could marry the widow and the child born to that union would go under the name of the previous husband. The property rights of the deceased man would also be passed on through the lineage.

But due to Naomi's age, this plan B was impossible; thus her despair. All hope was gone. Or was it?

In chapter 2 we observed how God used Ruth and Boaz to provide for her and help bring about a return to faith. At the end of the chapter, Naomi excitedly identifies Boaz as a "guardian-redeemer."

Hope was alive. A guardian-redeemer just could be Plan C. God has solutions that we may never consider.

When someone went through great loss, the nearest relative could engage in a redemption process. Leviticus 25 describes how these kinsmen-redeemers could purchase back land for those who, through poverty, had been forced to sell them. People could even be redeemed out of slavery.

A guardian-redeemer could marry a widow and through their union provide children that would continue the line of her deceased husband.

That was an option that Naomi apparently hadn't considered before... but she sure is thinking about it now!

God often surprises us with unexpected rescues. Due to my parents' finances, I worked my way through college. That required working full-time during the summers and holding numerous part-time jobs during the school year. But even with those wages and a few grants and scholarships, I sometimes agonized how I would come up with enough money to pay my college bills. On one particular occasion, I knew that I would have to drop out of school if I wasn't able to meet a coming financial deadline. So I called out to God and asked Him to graciously and supernaturally supply.

That weekend I took some teenagers to a seminar at an area church. While there, a woman backed into my car in the parking lot. Even though my old red Camaro was already riddled with dents, it smacked me down emotionally. As I looked at the bashed-in door, I wondered, "Is this the way God answers prayer? I ask for money for college and He lets someone crash into my car?"

Well, as matter of fact, that was exactly how God answered my prayer. The lady's insurance company gave me a check just in time to use it to pay my school bill. And, "coincidentally," the amount was just what I needed.

The car door?

I left it just the way it was. It still worked and the new design constantly reminded me that God would provide for me.

God's provisions had helped rebuild Naomi's faith and then the kindness of her relative, Boaz, opened her eyes to a possibility that engineered her return to hope. That's good but what was better was how she, through her proactivity, transformed the possibility into an opportunity.

Optimism grows when you start capitalizing on God-given opportunities

Let's pick up the narrative in the first four verses of chapter 3. "One day Ruth's mother-in-law Naomi said to her, 'My daughter, I must find a home for you, where you will be well provided for. Now Boaz, with whose women you have worked, is a relative of ours. Tonight he will be winnowing barley on the threshing floor. Wash, put on perfume, and get dressed in your best clothes. Then go down to the threshing floor, but don't let him know you are there until he has finished eating and drinking. When he lies down, note the place where he is lying. Then go and uncover his feet and lie down. He will tell you what to do.'"

Matchmaker, matchmaker, make me a match...

Following Naomi's advice must have been extremely difficult for Ruth. I was one of those guys who found it excruciating just getting up the guts to ask a girl out so I can only imagine the courage that this bold maneuver would take. The fact that Ruth proceeded shows her to be a person with a gentle spirit and steel will.

Can we also assume that she was not merely submitting to Naomi's counsel but also following her own heart? When she first met Boaz, she was flattered that a man of his position would take notice and show kindness to her, a foreigner. Then she enjoyed his company and generosity during their meal together. Would that count as a first date? (That is the question that Jodi and I ask ourselves about our first meal together at an A & W ice cream parlour. It just sort of happened; there was no advance plan. Does that count? I think so, and I keep a commemorative root beer mug in our cupboard as a keepsake). And when Ruth had returned home that night, she marvelled over Boaz's insistence that she return only to his fields. In the days that followed the attraction must have continued to grow.

Ruth set off in the dark toward the threshing floor. She looked good. She smelled good. She was man bait. She was also scared spitless. (Would you believe me if I told you that was a rare Hebrew word?) She darted through the shadows staying out of anyone's sight. Finally, she arrived to look for her love. From the background she saw him participating in the festivities.

It had been a long day for Boaz. Since it was now the end of the harvest season, his workers had brought the barley they had collected to this large area that had been pounded down so hard that it was like concrete. Then they used a rope to attach a big rock behind an ox. With the barley strewn on this threshing floor, the ox pulled the rock around and around, thus smashing the barley and allowing the grain to break free from the husks. At about five o'clock in the evening, a typical Far East wind picked up. When it was strong, they tossed the barley up into the air so that the light stuff would float way and the heavier grain would drop down to the floor. It, in turn, was scooped into piles and collected.

Boaz's men had worked hard and he rewarded them with a feast that celebrated the goodness of God's blessing during the harvest. It was a big meal with good wine, and the combination of work and food left them all exhausted. In order to protect their grain, they all slept right there.

After making sure everything was in order, Boaz located a private spot, spread out his garments, and fell asleep. Sometime that night, he awoke and sensed something was amiss. Was it the wind blowing over his cold, bare feet? No, it was something more. He felt a presence. Sitting up, he used the light of the moon to see a woman's form lying there at his feet.

Taken back, he whispered, "Who are you?"

"I am your servant Ruth," she whispered back. "Since you are a guardian-redeemer of our family, I am asking you to spread the corner of your garment over me."

Her request was as obvious to him as an outstretched diamond ring would be in our culture. In the second chapter Boaz had blessed Ruth with the words, "May you be richly rewarded by the Lord, the God of Israel under whose wings you have come to take refuge."

Returning Home

There is a literary link between these two verses. In Hebrew, the word for *corner* in Ruth's request is the same word for *wings* in 2:12. Often when a man wanted to propose, he would come into a house, take the wing of his garment and put it over the woman he wished to marry. This was a symbolic way to demonstrate that the man was willing, in the act of marriage, to become the protector of his new wife. In the same way that God puts His protective wings around us, a husband is taking on that role in the home.

Ruth's message was clear. She loved Boaz and hoped to become his wife.

This was a bold, progressive move by a woman. And there was every possibility that the gambit would be disastrous. In the dark of night, Ruth held herself, perhaps anticipating shame and rejection.

But there was none of that. Instead, Boaz earnestly replied, "The Lord bless you, my daughter. This kindness is greater than that which you showed earlier: You have not run after the younger men, whether rich or poor. And now, my daughter, don't be afraid. I will do for you all you ask. All the people of my town know that you are a woman of noble character."

Can you imagine what he was thinking? Ruth had caught his eye the moment he'd seen her, and even before that he'd heard of this brave, loyal woman who had risked everything to come with Naomi to Israel. Boaz had observed her industriousness in his fields and enjoyed her personality in their interactions. He'd surely allowed his mind to dwell upon her beauty and virtue. But he, at his age, had never allowed himself to ponder a future with her. Ruth was an attractive young woman who could have pursued younger men, whether wealthy or poor.

In Boaz's mind, Ruth's favouring him was an act of extreme kindness. Isn't that one of the marks of a true love relationship? When both parties think the other is too good for them?

Yesterday I jokingly told my thin, younger wife, "You are my better half. I, in turn, am the bigger half. You're quality; I'm quantity." What isn't a joke is my extreme appreciation to God for allowing this wise, beautiful woman to be my wife. I get Boaz.

And Boaz, once again displaying his persistently spiritual side, asked God to bless Ruth for her sweet initiative. He softly assured her that she could relax; he would do all that she asked.

"But..."

But? Ruth, overjoyed with Boaz's reciprocation of love, didn't want there to be any "buts." Unfortunately there was still a major roadblock that stood between them and the fulfilment of their hopes.

Returning Home

Anticipation grows as you patiently wait for God to bless your initiatives

Boaz says, "Although it is true that I am a guardian-redeemer of our family, there is another who is more closely related than I. Stay here for the night, and in the morning if he wants to do his duty as your guardian-redeemer, good; let him redeem you. But if he is not willing, as surely as the Lord lives I will do it. Lie here until morning."

And that is what Ruth did. Excitement kept her from sleep. Might she actually get to marry this man of great standing in Bethlehem? But what if the other kinsman-redeemer, the one first in line, exercised his right to first claim? He, out of a lust for Elimelek's property, might do so even if he had no interest in Ruth herself. What kind of marriage would that be?

Early in the morning, before it would be possible for Ruth to be seen or recognized, they arose. He filled her shawl with six measures of barley and propped the bundle on her back. "We don't," he said with a smile, "want you to return to your mother-in-law empty-handed."

Ruth returned home and told Naomi everything that had been done and said. The large bundle of barley was a physical portrayal of how much they had been blessed.

Throughout this story, there are a number of subtle parallelisms. Here again is another one. Naomi had left

Bethlehem when there was a famine but returned during a harvest. She came back saying, "I'm totally empty, God has emptied me of everything," but now God through Boaz is making sure that she will not be empty-handed. Out of the famine, God is giving her a personal harvest and filling the empty places in her life with blessing.

But what will happen now? We are now at the most suspenseful part of the story. Will Boaz be the redeemer or the other man who is at the front of the line? We have to wait and see.

Ruth and Naomi had to wait and see. Naomi said, "Wait, my daughter, until you find out what happens." Then the cagey old woman showed her knowledge of the ways of men by adding, "The man will not rest until the matter is settled today."

Now Ruth and Naomi at least have hope. That is a major reversal, isn't it? When hope was lost love came through. In chapter two we saw the return of faith. In this chapter we have, through a heart-touching romance, seen the return of hope.

This is a love story that displays the love God has for you

Don't you love a good love story? This is a very good love story and *it's a bigger love story than you may think.*

It's a love story that displays the love between Ruth and Boaz.

But it's bigger than that...

It's a love story that displays the love God has for Naomi, Ruth and Boaz.

But it's bigger than that...

It's a love story that displays the love God had for his people during the period of the judges.

But it's bigger than that...

It's a love story that displays the love God has for all people during all time.

Can anything be bigger than that?

The guardian-redeemer in the book of Ruth is a type of the future Redeemer who would come into the world and pay the purchase price to buy us out of slavery and become our bridegroom.

Genealogies are more than dusty historical records of names. They show God's love for people. He knows us by name. (He knows yours!) They show God's channeling His redemptive plan through human history. And they also show the ancestry of the Messiah.

In Ruth it is seen that not just anyone could step into the role of a kinsman-redeemer. And the same was true of the Messiah-Redeemer.

First, the Redeemer must be blood related. John 1:14 says, "The Word became flesh and made his dwelling among us. We have seen his glory, the glory of the One and Only, who came from the Father, full of grace and truth." In the incarnation, Jesus Christ became one of us. He was the second Adam (1 Cor. 15:45).

Second, the Redeemer must be able to redeem. First Peter 1:18-19 says, "For you know that it was not with perishable things such as silver or gold that you were redeemed from the empty way of life handed down to you from your forefathers, but with the precious blood of Christ, a lamb without blemish or defect." And in Titus 2:13-14, we read, "Jesus Christ gave himself for us to redeem us from all wickedness and to purify for himself a people that are his very own, eager to do what is good."

Third, the Redeemer must be willing to redeem. And because of Christ's love for us, that was exactly God's desire. John 3:16 says, "God so loved the world that He gave His only begotten Son..." And Ephesians 1:7-8 adds, "In him we have redemption through his blood, the forgiveness of sins, in accordance with the riches of God's grace."

Personalize all of this and you will discover that *this is a love story that displays the love God has for you.* Nothing is bigger than that!

Place yourself at God's feet and ask for his grace. Allow the Redeemer to cover you with His wing.

Returning Home

In his song, "*My Redeemer is Faithful and True,*" Steven Curtis Chapman says,

> My Redeemer is faithful and true.
> Everything He has said He will do.
> And every morning His mercies are new.
> My Redeemer is faithful and true.

Here's the big idea that you will want to remember: *God helps you return to hope when you capitalize on the opportunities He lovingly provides.*

The Side Story...

The Next Christmas

Sean held up two pieces of the Nativity set. "Your dad really made these? They are incredible!"

"Yes, he did," Emily said. "He could do anything with wood. In the carpentry trade, there are those who are known as framers and finishers. Framers get construction projects done fast and efficiently. Finishers, on the other hand, are artists that care about every detail. Dad was a finisher."

"Considering how you turned out, it appears that he was also a finisher when it came to parenting."

"Oh, Sean, you are so sweet. Daddy would have loved you as much as my mom does."

"Wow. Considering how much of a cupid she was, that is quite a bit. Once she determined we were right for each other, we had no choice but to get married."

"That's right, bub. And if you try to back out, she'll come after you with my dad's shotgun."

Emily paused and then said, "Setting up all the Christmas decorations was something that Daddy and I always did together. Until you, I wouldn't have considered doing it with anyone else."

Returning Home

The sun shining through the windows made his blue eyes sparkle. "Thank you, babe," he said. "That means so much to me. I hope to be a godly husband just like your dad was a godly parent. Say, do you think we could include this Nativity set somewhere among the wedding decorations? Maybe it could even be by the unity candle? Your dad won't be there to give you away but this could still represent his presence."

Emily hugged her fiancé tight and whispered into his ear, "That would be wonderful. Thank you so much."

The polished Nativity pieces were featured prominently in both the Christmas with her family and their December 30th wedding. To some measure, it felt like her dad was there; but even more, she felt the presence of her loving heavenly Father.

EPISODE FOUR

RETURNING TO FAITH

RUTH 4:1-13

Everybody loves a happy ending.

We especially want a happy ending for Naomi and Ruth. The trails and travails of these dear women have captured our heart. At the beginning of their story, we hurt with them. And now that there is the possibility Boaz might be a redeemer, we hope with them. Part of the reason is because, on some level, we relate. We've been through our own difficult times. And even now, some of us are back in Moab, experiencing loss and brokenness.

A while back I read a story about speaker and writer, Chip Ingram. He described a time when at the age of twenty-one and due to his faithfulness to Christ, he lost the love of his life. As he saw her walking away from him on the arm of another man, he was devastated.

He writes,

> I could not believe my eyes. I felt rage, betrayal, and complete disillusion welling up in the depths of my soul. I asked God, "How could you let this happen to me after the great sacrifice I made for you, and how could you let her get hooked up with him?" I knew this player's intentions with girls. I'd heard all about his former conquests. I knew how he mocked my faith in God.
>
> As I walked across campus, I was rethinking whether this God I'd come to know was worth following. I was questioning if I wanted to continue in a relationship with a God who rewarded great sacrifice and commitment with such injustice and pain. I was questioning the character and trustworthiness of God. I remember mumbling certain phrases to myself as I made that long journey to my dorm room. "I feel so angry. Why do the people that don't walk with God get all the good stuff? And, why, instead of getting what's good, do I get what's lousy? Why is life so unfair? Why God? Why God did you allow this to happen?"[6]

Sounds a bit like the first chapter of Ruth, doesn't it? There we saw Naomi going through an incredibly painful period of her life. She lost her home, husband, sons, and livelihood. On the inside, her catastrophe had cracked her spiritual and emotional foundations. Her faith, hope, and joy died along with the key people in her life and she returned to Bethlehem a husk of the woman she once was.

As Chip Ingram read his bible, God gently touched him through Psalm 73. In the psalm, Asaph, a key choir leader, describes his grief and bitterness. Then there's a shift in the psalm where Asaph lifts his eyes to the Lord and says, "Yet, I am always with you." Chip said,

> This passage and the verses around it, really ministered to me, and its application is that, like the psalmist we need to realize that when a raw deal comes our way, we have God. We may not have a job anymore. We may not have a house or an inheritance or a relationship, but we can proclaim to the Lord, "I have You, and You hold me by your right hand. You guide me. You promise to be my portion. You are always with me, regardless of the circumstances which I find myself." And when we worship as Asaph did, we gain an eternal perspective of what is real wealth and what is not. That same eternal perspective helps us endure the lost relationship, the

lost money, the gossip, the betrayal, the painful disappointments. The eternal perspective keeps the raw deal from destroying our lives. That raw deal does not have the power to destroy us unless we turn bitter, get vengeful, or let it eat us up. We do live in a fallen world where bad things happen to good people and good things happen to bad people, but even though our world is fallen, it is subject to its maker. God is in control. God allows raw deals, but He promises to work them ultimately for our good.[7]

It's the word of Romans 8:28, "For we know that all things work together for good to those who love God and are called according to his purpose." The book of Ruth teaches us that God has a way of working things out. After the bitter return in Ruth chapter 1, there was a return to faith in chapter 2 and a return to hope in chapter 3. And now in the final chapter we get to see a return to joy. God is working things together for good.

The Pursuit of the Redeemer

Chapter 4 begins with the word, "Meanwhile." The previous night the couple had declared their devotion for each other and Boaz had pledged to do all he could to fulfill the role of a guardian-redeemer. This was ratified by Naomi, who had assured Ruth that Boaz would definitely act with honor and haste.

When Ruth and Boaz left the threshing floor, she went to Naomi and he went to the town. He had a lot of preparations to do before morning, when Bethlehem would awake and the hub-bub would begin.

The next time we see Boaz he is at the gate of the city. Even now, if you travel through these ancient little villages of that area, you will observe that the streets are narrow and the houses and shops are tucked close together. The only real place to meet was in a public square by one of the gates. And since Boaz knew the habits of the town well, he rightly presumed that his rival kinsman-redeemer would probably come through a particular gate. So, there Boaz waited until his relative came.

We don't know the individual's name. The writer probably shielded the man's shame by not mentioning it. When he did arrive, Boaz invited him over to sit beside him. Then he gathered ten of the town elders to join them for a matter of business. Since it was obvious that something big was going on, other people also gathered around to watch.

Boaz says, "As I am sure you know, Naomi has returned from Moab completely destitute and now she must sell the one remaining field that belonged to her husband, Elimelek. Since you are the closest relative to have the option of purchasing it, I thought I would bring it to your attention and suggest that you obtain it. If you choose not to, I, the second in line, would like to do so. These elders sitting here will serve as witnesses to whatever decision you would like to make."

It's almost like a game of Monopoly. You roll the dice and are excited to see that you have landed on Boardwalk. Without much thought, you immediately say, "I'll buy it."

And that's what this man says. The storyteller likely imagines his listeners groaning at this point because that's not how the story is supposed to end. And we agree, don't we? We've grown to love Ruth and Boaz. We've witnessed their midnight romance. We want them together. If this man gets the field, he also gets Ruth. It's a package deal. This is a terrible twist.

But the script was no surprise to Boaz. He's a prudent man who's acting with integrity. But he is also a wise man who has thought out his approach. He now shares another bit of information that apparently this first kinsman-redeemer hadn't considered.

Looking his fellow bidder in the eye, Boaz says, "Now, you recognize that in the day you purchase the property, you'll also bear some responsibilities along with it. As the guardian-redeemer, you don't just acquire that property. You also assume the responsibility to take care of Naomi, marry Ruth, and bear children through her."

Now the first kinsman-redeemer sits in silence, thinking through the consequences of all this. This had now become an incredible financial investment that might not bear any return. You see, property rights in Israel always went back to the family members, and even if a piece of property was purchased by someone else, when the year of Jubilee came, it would revert back to the person that previously owned it so all that property could stay in the family line.

He had been thinking, "Since Naomi has no husband or sons, I'll be able to take this property and keep it for myself. My property is going to get so much bigger. I'm not only going to have my own part, I'm going to have all of this as well and I'll be able to keep it forever."

But the Ruth factor changes the equation. Now he recognizes that he will pay out the money for the field, provide financially for Naomi and Ruth, and then, if a son is born, have it all placed in his name. It would return to the line of Elimelek.

You land on Boardwalk and want to buy it until you realize that it will take all of your money, and if you land on someone else's property soon after, you just might be out of the game. What do you do?

If you want even more perspective, return to Deuteronomy 25— a passage that we looked at before. Starting with verse 5, we read, "If brothers are living together and one of them dies without a son, his widow must not marry outside the family. Her husband's brother shall take her and marry her and fulfill the duty of a brother-in-law to her. The first son she bears shall carry on the name of the dead brother so that his name will not be blotted out from Israel. However, if a man does not want to marry his brother's wife, she shall go to the elders at the town gate and say, 'My husband's brother refuses to carry on his brother's name in Israel. He will not fulfill the duty of a brother-in-law to me.'" And if there wasn't a brother-in-law, the custom was that the right went to a kinsman-redeemer.

Moving on to verse 8, we discover the next phase, "Then the elders of his town shall summon him and talk to him. If he persists in saying, 'I do not want to marry her,' his brother's widow shall go up to him in the presence of the elders, take off one of his sandals, spit in his face and say, 'This is what is done to the man who will not build up his brother's family line.' That man's line shall be known in Israel as The Family of the Unsandaled."

Finally coming to a decision, the man reaches down and removes his sandal. Not only doesn't he want the financial risk and family responsibilities, but he's most likely wrestling with prejudice. Ruth was, after all, a Moabite, a nationality most Israelites despised. There could've even been some superstition involved. Naomi had gone away a blessed woman, and she had lost everything. Her husband and sons had all died.

With all eyes on him, the man would disappear from history with one final act. He handed his sandal to Boaz and said, "I cannot redeem the field because I might endanger my own estate. Buy it yourself." The transferred sandal symbolically implied that he gave up his right to walk on that land.

According to Deuteronomy, the elders could have gotten Ruth and had her spit in the guy's face because he was acting in self-centeredness and not acting protectively in his role as a guardian-redeemer. But they kindly let him off the hook.

Can you imagine Boaz's joy?

He stands to his feet, looks at all the elders and the other people who had gathered, and loudly announces,

> "Today you are witnesses that I have bought from Naomi all the property of Elimelek, Kilion and Mahlon. I have also acquired Ruth the Moabite, Mahlon's widow, as my wife, in order to maintain the name of the dead with his property, so that his name will not disappear from among his family or from his hometown. Today you are witnesses!"

Redemption has occurred. Let the festivities begin!

With a festive, party flair, the elders and people take turns pronouncing rich congratulations and blessing upon Boaz. They ask God to bring fame to Boaz and make Ruth as fruitful as the greatest women in their nation's history.

These witnesses have just beheld two men acting as polar opposites. The first, acting in complete self-interest, wanted possession of land but backed off once he recognized that it would be a costly, risky investment. Boaz, on the other hand, operated in pure sacrificial love. He would gladly pay the redemption price so that he could be united with Ruth and have the privilege of caring for Naomi. Chapter 2 revealed that Boaz was already viewed as a man of high standing in the community but now the respect level for him skyrocketed even further. This was the kind of man deserving of praise, honor and fame and the people gave it gladly. They could also see Boaz's joy in Ruth and they shared his exuberance.

And can you imagine Ruth's excitement? Earlier parts of the story display the love and respect she felt for Boaz and now he would become her husband. She has been redeemed! What a reversal of fortunes. She goes from poverty to wealth, from loneliness to love, from worry to peace, from despair to hope, from field worker to first lady, from foreigner to citizen, and from stigmatized to significance. She is no longer "Ruth the Moabitess;" she is now "Ruth the wife of Boaz," a name she is proud to bear. And she has the added reward of knowing that Naomi, the woman to whom she had pledged loyalty, would now be adequately provided for.

Shortly after the town meeting, Boaz marries Ruth. And blessing comes quickly to the married couple. God enables Ruth to conceive and then provides a son. The women of the village become the cheerleaders for this further cause of rejoicing.

You, too, can share in the joy of redemption

Doesn't this remind you of our relationship with God? Isaiah 54:15 says, "For your Maker is your husband— the Lord Almighty is his name— the Holy One of Israel is your Redeemer; he is called the God of all the earth.

In the New Testament, Jesus is pictured as the bridegroom and the church, the collection of all believers, is His bride. That is why, in the words of Titus 2:12-15, "we wait for the blessed hope—the appearing of the glory of our great God and Savior, Jesus Christ, who gave himself for us to redeem us from all wickedness and to purify for himself a people that are his very own, eager to do what is good."

Redemption may merely mean "deliverance," but usually it refers to a deliverance accomplished by the payment of a price or ransom. Ephesians 1:7-8 says that in Christ, "we have redemption through his blood, the forgiveness of sins, in accordance with the riches of God's grace that he lavished on us with all wisdom and understanding." When our Lord Jesus Christ died on the cross he redeemed believers. He bought back that which was lost; he made it possible for us to be freed from the bondage and penalty of sin. A new family was created by the intervention of our great kinsman-redeemer—a family to which you, if you are a Christ follower, belong.

Joy grows in our life as you indulge in your union with your Redeemer. You can enjoy a deep, intimate relationship with Christ. The bondage and poverty of your past life has been replaced with freedom and fullness. *God helps you return to joy as you celebrate the Lord's redemptive work in your life.*

For all of eternity Christians will celebrate the price Jesus paid on the cross so that we, the church, could become His bride. Revelation 5:9 says,

> You are worthy to take the scroll
> and to open its seals,
> because you were slain,
> and with your blood you purchased for God
> persons from every tribe and language
> and people and nation.

Returning Home

Jesus Christ should be praised for His role as our Redeemer, and the church should be fruitful. The account of Boaz and Ruth is a reflection of the story of Jesus and us. Our goal is to glorify the Lord and be used by Him to multiply disciples.

The story does have a happy ending!

Oh, wait. The story isn't finished. It gets even better.

In an intriguing way, the attention suddenly shifts from Boaz and Ruth, to whom the son was born, back to Naomi, the exuberant grandmother. It is here that the celebration of joy hits its pinnacle. The women of the village shout, "Praise be to the Lord, who this day has not left you without a guardian-redeemer."

In the next episode we will study the significance of that and the eternal consequences of the birth of this baby...and another baby.

The Side Story...

The Next Christmas

Sean and Emily held hands as they watched Grandma Nancy hold their baby in her lap. As the elderly woman happily cooed, the little guy laughed baby chuckles that made everyone in the room join in the laughter.

They were all together for another Christmas—brothers, sisters-in-law and Emily's nieces and nephews. And the center of attention was her baby boy, Joshua. He was named after her father. It was a happy, joyful, "God is so good" family gathering. Father.

EPISODE FIVE

RETURNING HOME

RUTH 4:13-22, MATTHEW 1

Starting with the ancient Greek theater and then continuing with the Romans, one of the elements frequently used by the playwright was the chorus. Standing in the background as the actors took center stage, they would sing and sometimes speak. Their job was to provide introductions, give transitions, and emphasize what was being portrayed by the actors.

In the book of Ruth, the women of Bethlehem play, to some measure, the part of the chorus. We see them first in chapter 1 where they witness Naomi's return with Ruth. They stood there appalled and saddened as Naomi spewed out her hurt, loss, and disappointment with God.

They haven't been observed since that low point of tragedy, but now that we are in the triumphant final act, they are back on the stage.

That doesn't mean, of course, that they've been nonexistent. They watched Ruth the Moabitess, as she endured risk and hard work in the wheat fields. They probably whispered and gossiped when Boaz, one of the town's leading citizens, took an interest in Ruth and provided her safety and extra grain. And, of course, they witnessed Boaz aggressively exercise his role as a guardian-redeemer in order to obtain Ruth as his wife.

A baby in a lap...and a story of redemption

But now that a baby has been born to Boaz and Ruth, the ladies are here to celebrate and clarify God's grace toward Naomi. "The women said to Naomi: 'Praise be to the Lord, who this day has not left you without a guardian-redeemer. May he become famous throughout Israel! He will renew your life and sustain you in your old age. For your daughter-in-law, who loves you and who is better to you than seven sons, has given him birth.' Then Naomi took the child, laid him in her lap and cared for him. The women living there said, 'Naomi has a son!' And they named him Obed. He was the father of Jesse, the father of David."

Returning Home

From the commentary given by this feminine worship team, we learn several things. First, we discover that God is the one who gets the praise. The Lord's obvious presence may have been curtained off from earthly eyes, but it is obvious to all that it is the sovereign Almighty who has been managing people and circumstances for Naomi's welfare. Isn't it calming to know that God limitless love and power to rearrange the events of life so that we can experience His best?

Second, it is amazing to see that the baby boy is also identified as a guardian-redeemer. He is the one who will assure a future for Naomi and her family. God will use Obed to minster to Naomi and give her new life. He will bring her renewal, restoration and sustenance. His very name means "servant" and he will serve Naomi for the rest of her life.

In the Hebrew language, this passage has an interesting play on words. A literal translation of "he will renew your life" is "he who causes life to return [Hb. *Shub*]." This word for return was used negatively in in 1:21 where Naomi complained that the LORD "brought me back [Hb. *Shub*] empty." But now there is a complete reversal. Naomi had returned to Bethlehem with an empty life but through this child, God had returned to her a life of fullness. It reminds me of the prophet Joel writing about how God will restore the years the locusts have eaten.

God has a return for you, too. You can experience a renewed life full of restored joy and divine protection.

Third, Ruth is given special tribute. We've seen how much Naomi treasured her sons. The ladies proclaim that her daughter-in-law has treated her better than seven sons could. The number *seven* had special meaning to the people of God. It expressed completion or fullness. This takes us back again to Naomi's complaint in 1:21. There she spoke to the ladies about how she had returned "empty." Now she is full. Her return is complete.

Finally, this baby is called Naomi's son. Her role in raising him will be intimate. She will be a special loved one in the boy's life—and he in hers. She holds him close and for the rest of her life he will hold her close. He will be there to cherish, protect and provide for her.

Naomi's life is filled with joy.

When she returned to Bethlehem, these very ladies were the ones who used the actual meaning of her name to shout out, "Pleasant is back! Pleasant is back!" She rebuked them then and told them to call her "Bitter" instead.

That has all changed.

"Pleasant" is back! She has now completely returned.

In chapter 1,
Naomi returned in bitterness to Bethlehem.

Returning Home

In chapter 2,
there was a return to faith.

In chapter 3,
there was a return to hope.

In chapter 4,
there was a return to joy.

And now Naomi's return is complete.
She has returned home...to the heart of God.

Do you have a story of redemption?

Naomi's story is unique, but it is not isolated. At some point or another, most of us go through Naomi-type experiences. If that is where you are, please turn to God. He has a happy ending for you too. I can't tell you how or when or whether it is in this life or the next because this isn't a cookie-cutter script. But we can have full confidence that the final chapter will be a good one.

Perhaps you, like Naomi, have experienced tragedy. That is your chapter one. Don't let your life story end like that. To return from the devastation of deep loss, just head in the right direction and God will walk by your side and provide the help you need.

Now it is time for your chapter two. God will help you return to faith as you open your eyes to His faithfulness.

Now that your confidence in the Lord is coming back, it is time for chapter three. God helps you return to hope when you capitalize on the opportunities He lovingly provides.

Chapter four is where it really gets good! God helps you return to joy as you celebrate His redemptive work in your life.

Don't treat the book of Ruth as just an Old Testament story; make it yours. And let it not be a mere, theoretical concept, let it come alive in your life as it has in so many others.

After preaching a series on Ruth as a guest speaker, I received a letter from one of the church members who described her Naomi-like story. With her permission I have removed some of the parts that might embarrass others, and share it with you now.

Dear Pastor Sheveland

I have been where Naomi was. Well, I didn't lose my husband or children, but I was full and came back empty. I have felt just like Naomi. I was bitter and angry for the pain in my life. I didn't understand what God was doing. I was very much like Naomi. I remember crying out to God and saying, prove to me that I can trust you or I am walking away. I had lost faith. I had lost hope and I had lost joy.

God could have just taken me out right then and there, but my God is a compassionate God and He was definitely up for the challenge. He took me broken and all through the valley. It was a long hard journey. I experienced God in a way I never would have if this situation hadn't come into my life...

You see, I've learned that the only way out is through so God took me through. Like Naomi, he gave me a Ruth that stood by me through it all. I cannot tell how having that support made the pain bearable. You may be wondering, what could be so bad that took me to the point of almost walking away from the one thing I held close through all my life, God. There's so much I can't go into, but I can tell you that my family was falling apart, one betrayal after another...

God somehow through it all began to restore my soul and better my life, my marriage and my family. Just like Naomi He sent me a kinsman-redeemer and that is God Himself. He redeemed me.

That was her story of the redemptive work of God. Do you have one?

My mother grew up in a poverty-stricken family in a forest region of Wisconsin where my grandfather was a lumberjack. He was a hard worker, but he was also an alcoholic who had spent many of his years in the tavern owned by his mother. His alcoholism was distressing for the family. On the days he would get paid, my Grandma Curran would walk down the road and try to get to him before he got his paycheck. Otherwise, it would all go to alcohol.

One day, while driving drunk, he hit a child and killed him. Grandpa was put in prison, and my grandmother, perhaps because of the pain of the marriage and finance troubles, divorced him. It was the only way that she was going to get any money from the state to try to feed her kids. But her action caused her to feel a great deal of guilt. She kept it quiet, and when grandfather got out of prison, he moved back into the home. They weren't married, but they lived on. This only increased her shame.

When my aunt Ruth graduated from high school, she moved to the big town of Oshkosh, Wisconsin, found a job, and also got involved in a church. A year later my mom followed her path and her example. Finally, with the exception of grandpa, they were all there in Oshkosh and God, one by one, brought each of them to faith.

My parents met, went to Northwestern Bible College together, got married, had three children, and established a wonderful Christian home. There were many occasions when my Grandma Curran came to live with us in our home. She was a Christ-follower who regularly attended church, but she could never seem to break free from her painful, shameful past.

Returning Home

When her grandchildren got saved and followed the Lord in baptism, she would always be asked if she, too, would like to get baptized. But because she never felt worthy, she always refused.

Then God started doing a work of grace in her life, and He gradually convinced her that He was a God of grace, forgiveness, and second chances. Her past could be erased and she could have a fresh, new life of vitality. So finally, when one of my younger nephews decided to get baptized, she surprised all of us and said, "I'm going to get baptized with him." Before my little old, white-haired grandma was immersed, she asked the pastor to read Psalm 30:5, "Weeping may endure for a night, but joy cometh in the morning."

Don't despair. Joy is coming your way too. God writes the final chapter and if you are in His hands, you can expect to live "happily ever after."

So, are we finally to the happy ending of this story in the Bible?

No, it gets even better!

A baby in a manger and the ultimate story of redemption

The book ends with a genealogy—a genealogy that shows us that Obed, the Bethlehem baby would become the grandfather of King David himself.

And now we get the rest of the story. It runs right through the line of David and culminates in Jesus Christ.

Up until now, the book of Ruth has been a living, breathing illustration of what love and redemption look like. We've been treated to a demonstration of how deeply God cares for people and He shows it in His providence and steadfast, loyal love. Then all of a sudden, the writer tells us there's more to the story than we could have ever imagined. We've been looking at these past events but verse 17 fast forwards us into the future and gives us a long view. It also tells us one of the primary reasons this little book is part of Scripture.

"He, [Obed] was the father of Jesse, the father of David" (4:17). That's it.

This account is vital for us to have, because Ruth the foreigner, Ruth the one who pledged herself to her mother-in-law and her God, Ruth the one who came to Bethlehem from pagan Moab, is the great-grandmother of King David of Israel—the man after God's own heart. Here in the little town of Bethlehem, where King David's grandpa was born, David would also be born, and much later, the Messiah would come into the world in this very place.

The mention of David's line communicates so much. God providentially worked in the middle of a perverse, godless generation to preserve a godly family line through whom the Christ child would come. Decades

Returning Home

before David was born, our Sovereign Lord powerfully weaved the threads of history together and accomplished His purpose. God drew Ruth the Moabitess, to Himself, and she became faithful. And her faithfulness, along with that of her husband Boaz, laid the foundation for the faithful godly heritage that would become David's.

Here is another interesting detail. Ruth's name is mentioned in only one other place in God's Word—in Matthew chapter one. There it appears in the genealogy of Jesus Christ.

Contrary to their reputation for being dull, genealogies are cool lists. There are forty-one genealogies in the Bible. They show God's love for people, his control of history and the ancestry of the Messiah. We should not be surprised, then, to find that the New Testament opens with a genealogy. It displays the lineage of Jesus Christ himself.

This genealogy doesn't give every single one of Christ's descendants from Abraham on. We know this from comparing this list with other genealogies in the Old Testament. The words that are translated "father" can also mean ancestor in a more general sense. We also use our English word "father" in a similar way speaking of the "faith of our fathers." It is obvious that Matthew is giving this genealogy in a selected manner for the purpose of introducing the Lord Jesus Christ as the King of the Jews. This is undoubtedly the reason why the genealogy falls into such a neat pattern, a triad of fourteen generations apiece. But in keeping with the inerrancy of the Scriptures, every single entry is accurately given as a member of the lineage of the King of Kings.

Now, we would expect many of the names listed, for they were great leaders and courageous warriors—the types of people who changed the course of human history. Abraham was the father of nations, David was a courageous warrior and world leader, Solomon was the wisest person who ever lived, Jehosphat, Uzziah and Hezekiah were great kings, and Zerubbabel was one of the pioneers who brought the Jewish people back into their land after the Babylonian exile. We would assume people like these to be found in the lineage of God's Messiah.

But there are also names of common folk and even several, like Rahab the harlot or the conniving Tamar, who were notorious for their sins. Black sheep are able to get into God's family because Jesus was the lamb without blemish who died for the sins of the world. And there are Gentiles like Ruth—outsiders we wouldn't expect. Isn't the message clear? Jesus came for all of us, no matter what our past looks like.

God sent His one and only Son into this world to rescue us from brokenness and deliver us from the bondage of our sins. Romans 5:8 tells us that God demonstrated His love for us in that while we were still sinners, Christ died for us.

The good news of the gospel is that Jesus Christ came to save us from our sins and from an empty way of life. He came to rescue us, set us free, and bring renewal.

The point is this: *God has always been in the business of redeeming people.*

Long before our Redeemer came, God redeemed lives—not only in Israel but outside it as well. People who were assumed to be without hope and without merit, God redeemed, again and again. He does the same today. He can do the same for you.

The book of Ruth celebrates a baby born in Bethlehem—Obed, the redeemer, the renewer, the servant. Through his line, came the Messiah—the ultimate Redeemer, Renewer, Servant and Savior. Obed's birth brought joy to Naomi, Ruth, Boaz, and the people of Bethlehem, but Jesus' birth in a stable brought joy to the world.

> Joy to the world, the Lord is come!
> Let earth receive her King;
> Let every heart prepare Him room,
> And Heaven and nature sing,
> And Heaven and nature sing,
> And Heaven, and Heaven, and nature sing.

Joy to the earth, the Savior reigns!
Let men their songs employ;
While fields and floods, rocks, hills and plains
Repeat the sounding joy,
Repeat the sounding joy,
Repeat, repeat, the sounding joy.

No more let sins and sorrows grow,
Nor thorns infest the ground;
He comes to make His blessings flow
Far as the curse is found,
Far as the curse is found,
Far as, far as, the curse is found.

He rules the world with truth and grace,
And makes the nations prove
The glories of His righteousness,
And wonders of His love,
And wonders of His love,
And wonders, wonders, of His love.

Isn't it time for you to come home?

As mentioned at the beginning of this book, the story of Ruth is a prequel to the advent of Jesus Christ. He is the Redeemer. No matter how much you have lost, God

Returning Home

can restore. No matter how far you have gone, you can come home.

Zechariah, the father of John the Baptist, made this prophecy regarding Jesus, the Messiah: "Praise be to the Lord, the God of Israel, because he has come to his people and redeemed them. He has raised up a horn of salvation for us in the house of his servant David" (Luke 1:68—69).

Jesus went on to die on the cross so that you could be saved and experience redemption. God's desire is that people return to Him.

God helps you return home spiritually when you embrace the Savior. This happens on the relationship level when you turn to Him in repentance and acknowledge Him as *your* Lord and Savior. That is a one-time transformation that makes you God's child. But on the fellowship level, the opportunity comes repeatedly. Whether it is a tragedy like Naomi experienced, or a temptation, we tend to drift away from our Savior and the abundant life He offers. Whenever this happens, we need to return home to the heart of God. James 4:8 says, "Come near to God and he will come near to you."

Many happy returns!

The Side Story...

Christmas Sunday

When Pastor Brewer called and asked them to be part of a Christmas sketch that Sunday, Emily had been quick to accept. Sean was another story. Even after bribes and wifely pleas, it still took the "yes-you-will" insistence of Nana Nancy to make him acquiesce. He couldn't defy his sweet, but firm mother-in-law.

It was Christmas Sunday, and the church stage was set up to look like a stable area. Sean, struggling not to display his embarrassment, wore a bathrobe and had a towel on his head. He was Joseph. Emily, garbed as Mary, stood by his side. Between them and the audience was a manger containing Joshua in the starring role of baby Jesus.

In Emily's opinion, her son was a great little Jesus. She looked up and saw her proud mother in the front row and knew that she would agree.

For a while, everything was mere pageantry and then, suddenly, the spiritual significance grasped Emily's heart. She looked at her baby and thanked God for His generosity. Her child was a wonderful gift...but the greatest gift of all was the Lord Jesus Christ.

ABOUT THE AUTHOR

Dr. Ron Sheveland is the director of *I-Training* (www.i-training.info), a ministry that allows him to train pastors and church leaders around the world through international teaching trips and internet resourcing. He also serves the Lord as an author, church consultant, and special speaker. Ron is a graduate of Cornerstone University (B.A.) and Denver Seminary (M. Div. & D. Min.). He has pastored churches in Michigan, Colorado and California. For a decade he was the director of the *Converge Michigan*—a ministry that specialized in church planting and church revitalization.

Jesus Christ is the joy of his life. In Ron's words, "It is my passion to know God better and share that knowledge with others." Family is his next priority. Jodi and Ron treasure their marriage and partner in all their life endeavors—including ministry. They have been blessed with two children: Luke and Jessica.

You can befriend him on Facebook or contact him through RevShev@aol.com or www.i-training.info.

Some Other Books by Ron Sheveland

Discover Your Personal Mission explains a Biblical process that will help you discover your particular ministry niche. God has a wonderful adventure waiting for you; don't miss it! The Creator has designed and equipped you to be fruitful and fulfilled in a unique mission He has hand-picked just for you.

The Perfect Gift is a ten-chapter book co-written by Ron Sheveland and Robert Laidlaw. It gives head-and-heart reasons for why you will want to accept God's gift of eternal life and includes a simple description on how to do so.

The Potluck People is a humorous novel that has been collecting "5 Star" reviews. Every church has some quirky people. But at Meanwhile Baptist Church, there is an overabundance of offbeat personalities -- and their antics, both funny and frustrating, are a challenge for their young, new pastor, Mike Lewis, and his fun-loving wife, Sandy. *The Potluck People* is an unforgettable comedy peppered with moments of love, tenderness, and lives being changed.

Baptism & Communion— Appreciating God's Artistry. Baptism and the Lord's Supper are two stunning pictures painted by the Master Artist. Due to disagreements within the Christian Church as to the nature of these symbols, we sometimes allow the debate to sidetrack us from gazing at their enormous beauty. BAPTISM & COMMUNION is a short book that clearly explains the Biblical issues, but then goes on to explore many of the facets of God's artistry displayed whenever a baptism or communion service takes place.

~ ~ ~ ~ ~ ~ ~ ~

Dear reader,

If you enjoyed this book, please consider posting a review of it.

Thank you!

~ ~ ~ ~ ~ ~ ~ ~

---

[1] C. S. Lewis, *A Grief Observed* (New York: Bantam, 1976), 1–4.
[2] Ibid., 4.
[3] Ibid., 4-5.
[4] David Jackman, David, *Mastering the Old Testament,* (Nashville: Word, 1993), 321.
[5] Arnold Fine, "Letter in the Wallet," (*Reader's Digest*, September, 1985), 49-52.
[6] Chip Ingram, "Experiencing God When You Get a Raw Deal," 2007, <http://www.crosswalk.com/spirituallife/11557796/> (accessed October 26, 2007).
[7] Ibid.